W9-AYO-150

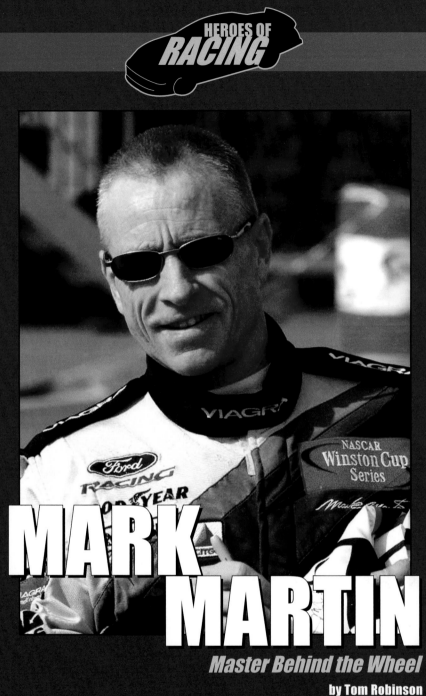

MARK MARTIN

Master Behind the Wheel

by Tom Robinson

Enslow Publishers, Inc.
40 Industrial Road
Box 398
Berkeley Heights, NJ 07922
USA
http://www.enslow.com

Library of Congress Cataloging-in-Publication Data
Robinson, Tom.
  Mark Martin : master behind the wheel / Tom Robinson.
     p. cm. — (Heroes of racing)
  Includes bibliographical references and index.
  Summary: "A biography of NASCAR sports star Mark Martin"—Provided by publisher.
  ISBN-13: 978-0-7660-3001-5
  ISBN-10: 0-7660-3001-6
 1. Martin,Mark, 1959—Juvenile literature. 2. Automobile racing drivers—United States—Biography—Juvenile literature. I. Title.
  GV1032.M36R63 2008
  796.72092—dc22
  [B]
                                              2007016077

Credits
Editorial Direction: Red Line Editorial (Bob Temple)
Editor: Sue Green
Designer: Becky Daum

Printed in the United States of America

10 9 8 7 6 5 4 3 2 1

CONTENTS

1 STILL GOING STRONG, 5

2 A DIRTY JOB, 13

3 MOVING UP, 21

4 GETTING STARTED, 29

5 TEAM SPORT, 39

6 WINNING STREAK, 49

7 MR. VERSATILITY, 57

8 HOMETOWN HERO, 71

9 TOUGH TO SAY GOODBYE, 80

10 MAKING CHANGES, 93

Career Statistics, 112
Career Achievements, 116
Chapter Notes, 118
For More Information, 123
Glossary, 124
Index, 126

Mark Martin hurried in and out of the pits. Martin and his team decided to add gas, but not to change tires, on each of his last two pit stops. As he worked his way up through the field to finish fourth in the 2006 Lenox Industrial Tools 300 in Loudon, New Hampshire, Martin put his years of experience to work. Would the few seconds saved in shorter pit stops be lost to the handling and traction that would be sacrificed on less-than-perfect tires?

Martin was working from the feel he had developed in more than

Mark Martin waits for his qualifying attempt for the 2006 Ford 400.

three decades on racetracks. Martin's feel for his car and his feel for the track guided him.

There are only a handful of NASCAR drivers who might know the New Hampshire International Speedway as well as Martin. Clearly there are none who know it any better than Martin.

He was there in 1993 when the track made its debut on the NASCAR Cup circuit with the Slick 50 300. Martin was still there and at every other stop on the NASCAR circuit for every race through the end of the 2006 season.

New Hampshire International Speedway became a special place for Martin. The track was the site of Martin's 500th straight Cup start. It was again the location when Martin became the fifth man in series history to start 600 straight races. On that special day, July 16, 2006, Martin cruised to a fourth-place finish.

SECOND CHANCE

The consecutive starts streak was the longest by any active driver. It began back in 1988 at the season-opening Daytona 500.

LONGEST NASCAR CUP CONSECUTIVE STARTS STREAKS
(through end of 2007 season)

1.	Ricky Rudd	788
2.	Rusty Wallace	697
3.	Terry Labonte	655
4.	Dale Earnhardt	648
5.	Mark Martin	621

PASSING THE MILESTONES

How Mark Martin performed in the races that marked milestones in his career

Milestone	Date	Track	Pole Position	Finish
100th straight	June 16, 1991	Pocono	1	3
200th straight	September 18, 1994	Dover	4	19
300th straight	November 16, 1997	Atlanta	9	3
400th straight	November 12, 2000	Homestead	11	3
500th straight	September 14, 2003	New Hampshire	33	28
600th straight	July 16, 2006	New Hampshire	13	4

The 1988 Daytona 500 was a second chance for Martin, who did well on the track as a young driver but ran into sponsorship difficulties that threatened his chance to ever get established in stock car racing's most prestigious series of races. That is when Jack Roush stepped in, choosing Martin to be the driver of the new NASCAR team he was starting.

Roush and Martin were still together in 2006, making it not only 600 straight starts for Martin, but 600 together as a racing team as well.

"It's been a great ride with Mark Martin for 600 starts now," Roush said days before the race in Loudon. "He's brought intensity, enthusiasm, great driving ability and integrity to the driver's seat, unlike no other driver that I can recall."[1]

Martin was clearly closer to the end than the beginning of his career when he hit the milestone. In fact, he had already been discussing possible retirement at times in each of the past two seasons. One thing that made retirement have to wait, however, was that Martin was still competitive.

On the day of his 600th straight start, Martin moved up one spot in the Chase for the lead in the Nextel Cup standings, going from sixth to fifth. Although he did not win a race or earn the pole as the leading qualifier in any race in 2006, Martin's consistency often kept him among the leaders in a given race and made him one of the most productive drivers during the course of the season.

ONE OF THE BEST

A total of 77 different drivers started NASCAR Cup races in 2006. There were forty-five drivers who appeared at least nine times. Out of that group, Martin ranked ninth in the final standings.

"As I started with this journey with Mark 19 years ago, I certainly didn't see the success and the number of wins we've had together," Roush said. "I also didn't see the term be-ing as long as it has, nor did I even consider that it would ever end."[2]

Martin was thankful for his owner's long-term com-mitment. Roush put Martin in position to have a long and distinguished career.

"That is a pretty big deal, and I am proud of that," Martin said. "I'm real proud of the history I have with Jack, and I'm proud that Jack kept me around this long."[3]

Any such streak by a NASCAR driver requires a bit of good fortune because of the dangers of the sport. Martin also brought with him toughness and dedication.

2006 STANDINGS IN THE CHASE FOR THE NEXTEL CUP

1.	Jimmie Johnson	6,475
2.	Matt Kenseth	6,419
3.	Denny Hamlin	6,407
4.	Kevin Harvick	6,397
5.	Dale Earnhardt, Jr.	6,328
6.	Jeff Gordon	6,256
7.	Jeff Burton	6,228
8.	Kasey Kahne	6,183
9.	Mark Martin	6,168
10.	Kyle Busch	6,027

DID YOU KNOW?

NASCAR stands for National Association for Stock Car Auto Racing.

Mark Martin (left) talks with car owner Jack Roush before the Daytona 500 on February 20, 2005.

"The thing that you've got to remember is that I've been lucky enough to, in a worst-case scenario, drive hurt and never had a sick day," Martin said. "That's a long time. Also, you've got to remember, I've driven awfully good cars. Otherwise that streak wouldn't be there."[4]

CONSISTENT CONTENDER

Martin would not take as much pride in the streak if it was just about getting to the starting line. Throughout the streak, he has also made it to the finish line often. How he has finished and where he has finished in the pack are what make Martin's career special.

"That doesn't mean you're the man by any means," Martin said of running in 600 straight races. "It's how fast you went in those 600 races that makes you the man."[5]

The nineteen-year run with Roush included 35 wins, 41 poles, and 373 finishes in the top ten. Martin appreciates the magnitude of those numbers.

"I'm actually very thankful for everything that I have been fortunate to accomplish," he said. "I'm thankful to everyone around me over the years that worked so hard for it, and I'm thankful to all of the fans out there who have stood by me for all of these years. I wish I was 25 and had that many ahead of me, but I'm still very thankful for everything that I have been able to do in my career. It really is a dream come true."[6]

The dream was nearly crushed in the 1980s when Martin could not put all the behind-the-scenes pieces together to allow him to be comfortable on the track, showing what he does best. That made it easy for Martin to keep going back to his relationship with Roush when talking about the meaning of one of his sport's most impressive endurance streaks.

"It says a great deal about Jack Roush, who basically gave me a second chance and a great opportunity to pursue my dreams," Martin said.[7]

Those dreams die hard, however. An expected semi-retirement in 2007 turned into a part-time schedule with a new owner. Martin completed the 2007 season with eleven top-ten finishes and placed twenty-seventh in the points standings.

MARK MARTIN

Birthdate: January 9, 1959

Birthplace: Batesville, Arkansas

Home: Daytona Beach, Florida

NASCAR Cup debut: 1981

Notes: Mark Martin was a full-time driver on the NASCAR Cup circuit in 1982 and from 1989 to 2006. He finished in the top eight in the final points standings in sixteen of eighteen seasons from 1989 through 2006. He won seven races in the 1998 season. In addition, he has had a successful career on the NASCAR Busch and International Race of Champions (IROC) series after earlier titles in the American Speed Association (ASA).

A DIRTY JOB

Many teenagers around the country dream of the arrival of their sixteenth birthday. One of the biggest reasons is the chance to begin driving.

There are states, however, that allow teenagers to start driving earlier. Arkansas, where Mark Martin grew up in the 1970s, allows fourteen-year-olds to drive with an instruction permit.

Martin was a bit ahead of schedule compared to many teen drivers. At fifteen, he was not just driving, he was racing. And young Mark was not just racing, he was winning. The truth is Martin got some training even earlier than laws in Arkansas allowed. In the 1970s, the safety value of car seats and seat belts was not as widely appreciated as it is now.

Julian Martin, Mark's father, was a truck driver who started his own successful trucking company in Batesville. He also sponsored a race team for local racetracks on the side. When his son was just five years old, Julian would stand Mark on his lap and let him steer the car on deserted country roads while Julian worked the gas and brakes.

Mark was comfortable behind the wheel as a fourteen-year-old and talked his father into building him a racecar that fall. The following spring, on April 12, 1974, Mark made his debut as a stock car driver at Batesville Speedway, a 3/8-mile oval dirt track in Locust Grove.

By his third race, Martin was in the winner's circle. He won the biggest race in his division in Arkansas at the end of his first year, taking the Arkansas State Championship at the Benton Speedbowl.

The Martins built racecars—and in the process, Mark's career—together. But

DID YOU KNOW?

Batesville is located on the White River in northern Arkansas, about 95 miles (153 km) north of the state capital of Little Rock. Batesville, the state's second-oldest city, had a population of 9,556 in 2006, according to Census Bureau estimates.

Ralph Garcia unloads a vintage racecar once driven by Mark Martin at the Arkansas Sports Hall of Fame Museum.

Mark's relationship with his father had some tough moments. Julian struggled at times with a drinking problem. By the time Mark was launching his racing career as a teenager, his father and mother, Jackie Estes Martin, had been divorced once and remarried. They ultimately got divorced again when Mark was eighteen.

Mark never could forget, however, how much his father did to help him get started in racing.

"You couldn't love a son more than he loved me," Mark was quoted as saying in Bob Zeller's book, *Mark Martin—Driven to Race*. "There was never any

HE SAID IT

"I'm not a carbon copy of my dad, thank goodness, or we would have lots of problems in my career and personal life. He was my hero and is the ultimate example of what the word 'man' means. But I'm a lot more calculated. I think things out a little more and have a lot more self-control than he had. There are things that don't measure up to him, either."

— Mark Martin
in Larry Cothren's "Racing's Steady, Consistent and Complex Superstar" at stockcarracing.com

question about that, even with all the things we went through and all the mistakes we made."[1]

TRAGIC NEWS

Mark was just finishing the Bud at the Glen race in Watkins Glen, New York, on August 10, 1998, when his father's private plane crashed in Nevada. Julian was killed along with Mark's stepmother, Shelley, and half-sister, Sarah.

A week later, Martin raced for the first time since his father's death. He could do nothing but sit in the car with tears in his eyes when the race was done. Although he led for fifty-seven laps, Mark finished fourth. As Mark sat there tormented, race winner Jeff Gordon was telling the media that he wished it was Martin and not him who had won that day's race in Michigan.

Only a week later, in his second race after the crash, Mark paid tribute to his father with the twenty-seventh victory of his career. The win was produced in dominant fashion, with Mark leading for 190 laps at Bristol.

"I want to thank the race fans for their sympathy, support, and love for our sport and our family," Mark said while addressing the crowd from Victory Lane. "I cried last week because I didn't get to dedicate a victory to my dad, Shelley, and Sarah. This one is for them tonight."[2]

As he circled the track on the last of those laps with the victory in sight, Mark was looking back, remembering all his father had done to create the opportunities on which he was now thriving.

Mark knew he picked up lessons from his early days driving with his father. "He could have been the best race driver ever, except he had a bit of a temper," Mark said.[3]

Julian may not have been able to turn himself into a racer, but he was a big part in making sure his son would succeed. Following his state championship in 1974, Mark started climbing through the various low levels of auto racing. Julian had been there as

MARTIN SYMPATHIZED WITH EARNHARDT, JR.

When Dale Earnhardt, Jr. lost his famous father, Dale Earnhardt, in an accident at the Daytona 500, Mark Martin was one fellow driver who could relate to Earnhardt, Jr.'s pain.

Although Julian Martin did not gain as many national racing fans as Dale Earnhardt, one of the all-time fan favorites among NASCAR drivers, he was a big part of his son's career.

Mark Martin remembered the feelings he had while moving on in his career while he watched Earnhardt, Jr. race in the 2001 season.

"I have more allegiance to Dale Earnhardt, Jr. than I do anyone else in relation to that, because I am a son who lost a father and I am really, really concerned with how he feels," Martin said that summer. " ... I know the pain he feels. Not all of it, because I didn't have to deal with it like he has. He still has to deal with it every day, every time he flips the TV on."

Because Earnhardt's death was such a huge story in the media, Martin said that when he watched Earnhardt, Jr., he at times was "wishing that I could shield him from some of that, because of the feelings that I have experienced myself, and I know it must be much worse for him."

In the process, Martin praised the media for showing discretion in how much it questioned Earnhardt, Jr. on the subject.

Mark Martin (left) shares a laugh with Dale Earnhardt, Jr. before the start of a race.

both his car owner and his crew chief from 1975 to 1979.

Mark was the Sportsman Division track champion at both Locust Grove and Benton Speedway in 1975.

Julian no longer shared the front seat with a new driver, but he was there in the garage and alongside the track as Mark's career developed. In just his third season, Mark was on to the V-8 Division, and he made the move from dirt tracks to racing on asphalt for the first time.

MOVING UP

The Batesville High School Class of 1977 gathered for its graduation ceremony. There was a notable absence. Mark Martin had earned his diploma, but he was elsewhere.

On his high school graduation day in Arkansas, Martin was busy in Springfield, Missouri. Martin set a track record that day while winning the Missouri Fairgrounds Championship.

The Missouri Fairgrounds Championship was one of three races Martin won that summer—his first season as a touring driver. He also won in Rockford, Illinois, and captured

Martin's career began to take off in the late 1970s, when he joined the ASA circuit.

the World Series at New Smyrna Beach Raceway in Florida.

Martin was no longer just one of the most accomplished Ozark Mountain stock car drivers, excelling on the many tracks of Arkansas and Missouri. He was ready to move up.

A BIG MOVE

With school behind him, Martin moved to Springfield, which became his base for traveling around the Midwest as part of the American Speed Association (ASA). He joined the ASA in time to run eleven races. He finished third three times and fifth two more times. When the season was done, he ranked fifth in the points standings and was named ASA Rookie of the Year.

The ASA gave Martin a chance to race against future NASCAR rivals Bobby Allison, Dick Trickle, and Rusty Wallace. Martin went from being the ASA's top rookie to being its top driver in just one year. He won the ASA overall points title each season from 1978 to 1980.

Along the way, Martin was earning respect as a clean driver. He would yield position to a faster car rather than forcing an opponent to risk a crash.

"Mark has been a good, clean driver all his life," Wallace said. "He's a quiet fellow. He has always gained a lot of drivers' respect. If he catches a driver, generally they'll get out of the way for him. Every time you catch Mark, he always moves over for you and gives you more room to operate. He has done that his whole life. He's a real straightforward kind of

DID YOU KNOW?

Alan Kulwicki, Kenny Wallace, Ted Musgrave, Robert Pressley, Johnny Benson, and Jimmie Johnson were among the drivers who followed Mark Martin by winning ASA Rookie of the Year honors before moving on to careers in NASCAR.

fellow. He never draws controversy. I love him to death."[1]

Martin opened the 1978 ASA season August 19 with his first victory on the circuit. He won $2,375 for taking the Redbud 300 at Anderson Speedway, not far from Indianapolis. He finished in the top ten in sixteen of the season's twenty races. The consistency he would show throughout his career was surfacing, as were the sometimes agonizing near-misses that went with the territory. Martin finished second six times during the 1978 season. He picked up his second win in October, leading sixty-nine laps on the way to a purse of $3,875 for taking the Buckeye 400 at Queen City Speedway in West Chester, Ohio, near Cincinnati.

At nineteen years old, Martin was the youngest season champion ever in the ASA.

Bill Davis, who went on to become a NASCAR team owner, ran Julian Martin, Inc. from 1975 to 1979 while Julian was helping launch his

DID YOU KNOW?

The American Speed Association (ASA) was a stock car racing sanctioning body that began in 1968 and was based in Pendelton, Indiana. The ASA started a national touring series in 1973 using late-model cars. The ASA often drew national cable television coverage, particularly from The Nashville Network from 1991 to 2004. The series split into two new tours in 2004.

ASA NATIONAL TOURING SERIES CHAMPIONS
(ASA reorganized and split into two tours after 2004 season)

1973 – Dave Sorg	1989 – Mike Eddy
1974 – Mike Eddy	1990 – Bob Senneker
1975 – Rodney Combs	1991 – Mike Eddy
1976 – Mike Eddy	1992 – Mike Eddy
1977 – Rodney Combs	1993 – Johnny Benson
1978 – Mark Martin	1994 – Butch Miller
1979 – Mark Martin	1995 – Bryan Reffner
1980 – Mark Martin	1996 – Tony Raines
1981 – Mike Eddy	1997 – Kevin Cywinski
1982 – Mike Eddy	1998 – Gary St. Amant
1983 – Rusty Wallace	1999 – Tim Sauter
1984 – Dick Trickle	2000 – Gary St. Amant
1985 – Dick Trickle	2001 – Johnny Sauter
1986 – Mark Martin	2002 – Joey Clanton
1987 – Butch Miller	2003 – Kevin Cywinski
1988 – Butch Miller	2004 – Kevin Cywinski

son's racing career. Davis saw a winning career taking shape with the combination of ability and motivation.

"Mark came by it naturally," Davis said. "His father was one of the most competitive people I knew and a perfectionist. He was very, very, very driven to succeed, and he instilled that in Mark. He taught Mark a strong work ethic at a very young age. There was a time when everyone thought Mark was just another rich kid that had guys working on his cars. While he

Team owner Bill Davis watches a race at Michigan International Speedway.

certainly had help, he was out there working as hard as anyone else."[2]

WINNING WAYS

Martin increased his wins, picking up three in 1979. He earned more than $10,000 for the first time with a win in the World Cup 400 at the I-70 Speedway in Odessa, Missouri. He also posted wins in Indiana and Minnesota.

Wherever he went with the ASA Tour, Martin was a threat to win. And he was getting better. He qualified as the best driver, taking the pole position, for ten of fifteen races in 1980. He turned the advantageous starts into five wins and five more second-place finishes. Martin won races at the Milwaukee Mile in May and August. He also won on two different tracks in Indiana and again at Queen City Speedway.

Other ASA drivers were having a hard time keeping up. In 1981, it was time for Martin to jump up again. He ran only twelve ASA races but picked up two more wins while he was trying to make the transition to bigger and better levels of competition.

MARK MARTIN'S WINNING ASA CARS

1978 — Chevrolet Camaro
1979 — Chevrolet Camaro
1980 — Dillon-Baker-AMSOIL Chevrolet
1986 — Miller American Racing Ford Thunderbird

GETTING STARTED

Mark Martin had clearly conquered racing's local and regional levels. It was time to move up again and take on the best stock car racers in the world.

Along with running part of the ASA schedule, Martin entered five NASCAR Cup races in 1981. He was testing the waters, setting up his move to full-time NASCAR racing for the 1982 season.

DABBLING IN NASCAR

The test went just fine. In his third NASCAR Cup race, Martin led

Mark Martin smiles at a group of cheering fans as he walks past Bobby Labonte.

qualifying to take the pole at Nashville International Raceway July 11, 1981, for the Busch Nashville 420. Martin avoided the car trouble that had left him dead last, stopped after just two laps during his previous start in Nashville. His Pontiac was still running at the end of the race, and he finished eleventh.

Martin improved in the remaining two chances he got in 1981, two weeks apart in September in Virginia. He won another pole at Richmond's Fairgrounds Raceway and took seventh at the Wrangler SanforSet 400. Then he qualified third on the way to a fifth-place finish at the Old Dominion 500 at Martinsville's Speedway.

The last start of the 1981 season had provided encouragement for the full-time try in 1982. Darrell Waltrip beat Harry Gant by nine seconds as they separated from the rest of the pack, which Martin led with his third-place finish.

ROOKIE SUCCESS

Martin was producing on the track as a rookie. He finished in the top ten in eight races. Results, however, were not enough. Martin was putting his own money into running his team, and problems with commitments from sponsors kept him from matching the on-track success with financial success.

Although Martin earned $115,600 in prize money for his NASCAR driving in his first full season, that was not enough to keep up with the costs of equipment and crew.

At the start of the season, the main sponsor was Apache Stove. By the time the season ended, sponsorship was changing, at times from race to race. Martin Racing was even listed as the main sponsor for his own car on three different occasions.

Even with the distraction of midseason sponsor changes, and the money problems that went with it, Martin actually improved on the track late in his rookie season. He

1982 NASCAR POINTS LEADERS

A total of 123 drivers raced at least once in the 1982 NASCAR Cup series and 50 raced at least five times. Darrell Waltrip won twelve races and the points title. The top fifteen in the final standings were:

1.	Darrell Waltrip	4,489
2.	Bobby Allison	4,417
3.	Terry Labonte	4,211
4.	Harry Gant	3,877
5.	Richard Petty	3,814
6.	Dave Marcis	3,666
7.	Buddy Arrington	3,642
8.	Ron Bouchard	3,545
9.	Ricky Rudd	3,537
10.	Morgan Shepherd	3,451
11.	Jimmy Means	3,423
12.	Dale Earnhardt	3,402
13.	Jody Ridley	3,333
14.	Mark Martin	3,042
15.	Kyle Petty	3,024

Martin races the No. 2 car in the 1983 Daytona 500.

finished tenth in his next-to-last race, then jumped up to fifth in the season-ending Winston West 500 at Riverside International Raceway in California.

PART-TIME DRIVER

When Martin could not pay to keep his team together, his fourteenth-place finish in the overall points standings and second-place finish among rookies meant nothing. He had to tear his team apart, selling off all his equipment in 1983. Martin occasionally filled in for other owners, but his full-time ride on the highest level of stock car racing was gone.

"In 1982, the sponsor that had been on the side of the car six months had not been paying its share of the bills," said Steve Peterson, who was Martin's crew chief in 1981. "Mark saw his dad going bankrupt and his mom using up all her savings just to continue on in '82. That was very hard on Mark from an emotional sense."[1]

Martin spent the 1983 season as a fill-in. He managed to have a car to drive in sixteen different races, but he was in and out of different models, driving Buicks, Chevrolets, and Oldsmobiles. He raced for four different owners and five different sponsors.

Although he was becoming auto racing's version of a pinch hitter, Martin kept up respectable performances on the track.

He qualified in the top ten in four of his first six races and managed three top-ten finishes for the season, including a tie for his best to date, a third-place finish in the TranSouth 500 in Darlington, South Carolina.

DID YOU KNOW?

Geoff Bodine was named NASCAR Rookie of the Year in 1982 when Mark Martin was second.

BACK TO ASA

Without a team and sponsor to race for and bring some stability to his career, Martin practically had to begin again. He went back to ASA in 1984. For two seasons, he did not make a single NASCAR start, and he even had to work his way back up the ranks of the ASA.

Mark Martin went two years without racing in a single NASCAR event in the mid-1980s.

While bouncing back and forth to NASCAR in 1983, Martin did not finish in the top four in any of his seven ASA starts. Running a complete schedule in 1984, he moved back to fourth in the points standings and picked up one win in the Coca-Cola Badger 300 at Slinger Speedway in Wisconsin.

"I gave up on it and just went where I could make a living," Martin

MARK MARTIN'S CAREER ASA STATISTICS

Starts: **143**

Pole Positions: **40 (4th best all-time)**

Wins: **22 (6th best all-time)**

Podium (Top Three) Finishes: **59**
(7th best all-time)

Top-Five Finishes: **80**

Laps Led: **4,690 (7th best all-time)**

Money Earned: **$432,834**

said. "That's what I do, is race, and I went where I could go and make a living and win races."[2]

Martin lost his usual consistency and had to settle for fourth in the standings despite winning four times in 1985. He won a pair of 400-mile races in Indiana late in the season, back at Anderson Speedway, the site of his first ASA win, and Winchester Speedway, where he picked up $13,685.

Peterson, who had been on Martin's crew for the first three ASA points titles, was with him again on the return to the Midwestern series.

"When Mark returned to ASA, it was very difficult on him emotionally," Peterson said. "He had been to the top of the mountain and had seen the other side, then fell back down and had to crawl back up. That's difficult on anybody. It changed Mark from being more of an outgoing personality to probably a little more introverted personality. He was definitely more critical of himself."[3]

CHAMPION AGAIN

With people such as Peterson at his side, Martin climbed the mountain and again had a view from the top of ASA in 1986. He was once again the top driver in that circuit and getting a chance to test himself in NASCAR.

Martin did not just win in 1986, he won often. In fifteen ASA starts, he won five times, took second three times, and took third twice. He started seven races from the pole position and won $104,740 on the ASA circuit.

Bouncing between series did not seem to hurt Martin.

Less than a month after finishing twenty-second at Charlotte in a NASCAR race,

DID YOU KNOW?

For much of Mark Martin's career, NASCAR's top racing series was known as the Winston Cup. The series debuted as Strictly Stock in 1949 and was known as the NASCAR Grand National from 1950 to 1970. A sponsorship agreement changed the name to the Winston Cup from 1971 to 2003. The series became known as the Nextel Cup beginning with 2004.

Martin picked up his first ASA win of the season in the Coors Light 300 at Madison International Speedway in Wisconsin. His best NASCAR finish was eleventh at the Delaware 500 at Dover on September 14. Martin returned to ASA and picked up his last two wins of the season in back-to-back races at Michigan and Winchester.

The big finish made it clear that Martin was again the series champion.

Mark Martin made the move from American Speed Association to full-time racing in the Busch Series, NASCAR's second-highest level, in 1987. All Martin seemed to need to get back to work in the NASCAR Cup series was the security of a strong commitment from the ownership and sponsorship of a race team.

Jack Roush was getting ready to move full time into the Cup series as he tried to make a bigger impact in the sport. The only thing he needed was a number-one driver to trust with the future of his team.

Martin exchanges hats with his son Matt as they celebrate a victory in 1999.

Martin talks with team owner Jack Roush in the garage area at Talladega Superspeedway.

Martin and Roush found each other. They also found a friendship that would last a lifetime.

"All through my life I've had people who were influential in my life," Martin said in a 2002 interview. "Today, it happens to be Jack Roush, because he's the one I come in contact with the most. My dad's gone, and I don't come into contact every day with a lot of people I had been in closer contact with. Jack is just so driven and so dedicated and so brilliant; so smart. He has an ability to analyze situations and problems and really understand them and understand how to address them."[1]

Together, Martin and Roush formed a winning team that lasted nearly two decades. When they finally broke apart the team following the 2006 season, they had put together nineteen straight seasons of racing, the only owner-driver team to remain together in the NASCAR Cup series through that entire period.

A TYPICAL NASCAR CREW

An example of the various assignments for working on Mark Martin's racecar on a typical race day in 2006:

Crew Chief	Pat Tryson
Car Chief/Front Tire Carrier	Todd Zeigler
Team Engineer	Mike Janow
Tire Specialist/Windshield	Jim Davis
Motor Man/Gas Man	Rick Machinski
Tire Specialist/Catch Can	Dave Nichols
Jack Man	Andy Rugger
Rear Tire Carrier	Will Smith
Shock Specialist/Spotter	Mike Senyitko

Martin was among the top eight in the final NASCAR Cup standings every year from 1989 to 2000. Continuing a part-time schedule in the Busch Series, Martin won just about one-third of the races he entered there from 1993 to 2000, taking the checkered flag in 38 of his 115 starts.

Martin had planned to end his full-time commitment to Cup racing at the end of the 2005 season, but Roush needed him. The Roush Racing team was going through a transition, and Martin's stability for one more season would be a big boost.

Remembering the way Roush was there when Martin's career so badly needed someone like him, the driver said yes to one more season.

CLIMBING BACK UP

Martin started just one NASCAR Cup race in 1987 and was out early with engine trouble. He did, however, build his reputation by racing on NASCAR's Busch Grand National level.

The drivers and cars are clearly at the center of attention in all NASCAR racing, but like any other sport, a team that works well together is necessary for success. Martin learned that during his early struggles to establish himself on stock car racing's highest level.

Martin won three Busch races in 1987. His win at Dover that year got the attention of Roush, who was preparing to start his own Cup team for the 1988 season. Roush hired Martin as his driver, starting the process of putting together a team that went on to win thirty-five Cup races and finish second in the final standings four times.

"Mark is one of the best drivers I've ever been around," Roush said. "He's talented, he's competitive,

A WINNING CREW

Mark Martin and his crew with the Roush Racing team won a NASCAR Cup race together for the last time October 10, 2005, in the Banquet 400 at Kansas Motor Speedway.

The contributions of the crew were easy to spot that day, from strategic moves made by crew chief Pat Tryson to a 13.6-second pit stop for fuel and four tires with the lead at stake late in the race.

"Those guys are my heroes," Martin said. "They help put me in front and then they kept me there. I asked each and every one of those guys to come back this year and they did and then on Sunday they put me in position to win the race. They got me there and kept me there. All I had to do was drive that thing. I can't say enough about those guys that go over the wall."

The flawless pit stop with a win on the line caught Martin's attention. "With all the pressure in the world on them, those guys were able to get in there and not only give us a good stop, but with the pressure at an all-time high, they gave their best stop and that's the mark of a championship-caliber team."

Crew members work on Martin's car during a pit stop.

and he has a good racing IQ. He doesn't make many mistakes."[2]

BUILDING A TEAM

The scene at a NASCAR press conference is predictable. The winning driver thanks his owner and his sponsors. He praises the work of the crew that gave him a great car to drive that day.

The simple truth is that each driver understands he cannot win without the parts of that team. By being part of one team longer than any of his rivals, Martin probably developed a deeper appreciation of the support. As he neared the end of his run with Roush Racing, Martin was happy that changes were not made much earlier in the process.

"For me, I got so invested in this program that it would've been ridiculous to bail at some point, you know, 10 years ago or so," Martin said. "We built this together, on each other's backs, holding hands, when things weren't good and things needed a lot of work, when we needed to learn a lot and each of us needed a lot of learning. At this point, I would be afraid to think about what might've happened if I had chosen to do something else."[3]

As he prepared to move on to a new team, Martin hinted that he could picture working with Roush Racing again in the future. He also made it clear that the team would always be a part of who he was as a racer.

"Instead of being emotional and broken-hearted, I'm more philosophical like, 'This has been awesome,'" Martin said. "It's been great for (Roush). It's been great for me. As far as I'm concerned I'll always be number six, and I think a lot of people will feel the same way."[4]

The prospect of racing for a different team in a different car with a new number is admittedly odd for Martin to picture. "Just because I stayed in the 6 car 19 years doesn't make it wrong for me to move on, it just makes it weird. It does make it weird, but it doesn't make it a tragedy," he said.[5]

In their last season together, Martin raced a Cup car and a Busch car and won six truck races, all while displaying the number 6. "There's some kind of karma there," Jack Roush said after Martin won his final truck race for the team. "I'm not sure what all that

THEY SAID IT

"There's no smarter driver in NASCAR than Mark. I've been around him for a long time and I really admire him. He's not loud and flashy, and he doesn't call a lot of attention to himself. I guess that's why he doesn't often get the credit he deserves. He just quietly goes about his business, and he sometimes tends to get overlooked. But I guarantee you, he's as good as anyone in the sport."

— former teammate Jeff Burton

means, but it's pretty special. Mark is leaving Roush Racing, but he's not leaving Jack as a friend. We'll be friends as long as we live, I'm sure."[6]

Martin stands next to his new Ford after a press conference to announce his team will be sponsored by Viagra in 2001.

6

WINNING STREAK

Mark Martin was on a two-race winning streak and in contention for a third straight when a loose wheel caused him trouble in the 1993 Bud 500 at Bristol International Speedway in Tennessee.

At one point, Martin fell two laps behind on the .533-mile track, which was the second smallest on the NASCAR Winston Cup circuit.

The Cup series featured three races on three different tracks in August 1993. Martin had already won on the road course at Watkins Glen and on the two-mile superspeedway at

Michigan International Speedway. Martin's streak was not done yet. After averaging less than 85 miles per hour through the many turns at Watkins Glen and almost 145 miles per hour cutting loose at Michigan, he needed a different driving style at Bristol.

"Bristol can be crazy," Martin said of the challenges of driving on a track where there is not much room to maneuver. "I've always said it is like flying a jet fighter around the inside of a basketball arena, and try that with 42 other jets doing it at the same time. It can get really intense, and it takes a great deal of patience by everyone. You just have to hope that you run well and that you can stay out of all the trouble,

Martin poses with members of the Roush Racing team before a race in 1993.

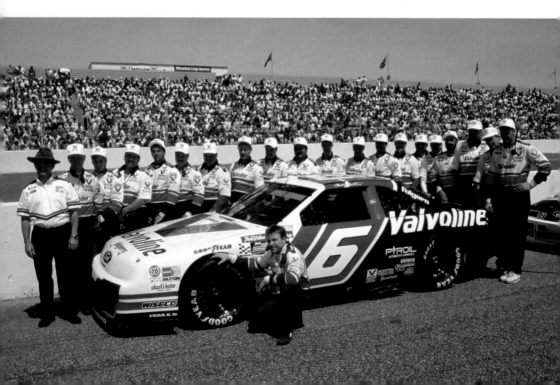

which isn't always easy to do."[1]

Martin came from behind to ruin what had been a nearly perfect day for Rusty Wallace.

Wallace led for 409 of the first 488 laps of the 500-lap race. He was mostly unchallenged until Martin attacked the high-banked oval and took the lead with twelve laps to go. Wallace kept trying to regain the lead, but Martin held him off.

WINNING STREAKS
The drivers who have won four straight NASCAR Cup races during the modern era (since 1972) include:

Cale Yarborough	1976
Darrell Waltrip	1981
Dale Earnhardt	1987
Harry Gant	1991
Bill Elliott	1992
Mark Martin	1993
Jeff Gordon	1998

After 500 laps and nearly 267 miles of racing, about one-seventh of a second separated the top two drivers. "It's not a big moral victory leading the most laps," Wallace said after the disappointing defeat.[2]

Martin had the closest and hardest-fought victory in what became one of NASCAR's most

MARK MARTIN'S STREAK

FIRST WIN:
BUDWEISER AT THE GLEN
Date: August 8, 1993
Site: Watkins Glen
International road course,
Watkins Glen, New York
Margin of victory: 3.84 seconds
Starting position: 1st
Laps led: 47

SECOND WIN:
CHAMPION SPARK PLUG 400
Date: August 15, 1993
Site: Michigan International
Speedway, Brooklyn, Michigan
Margin of victory: 1.28 seconds
Starting position: 12th
Laps led: 81

THIRD WIN: BUD 500
Date: August 28, 1993
Site: Bristol International
Speedway, Bristol, Tennessee
Margin of victory: 0.14 seconds
Starting position: 1st
Laps led: 67

FOURTH WIN:
MOUNTAIN DEW
SOUTHERN 500
Date: September 5, 1993
Site: Darlington Raceway,
Darlington, South Carolina
Margin of victory: 1.51 seconds
Starting position: 4th
Laps led: 178

amazing streaks of the last thirty-five years. The winning streak went on into September and another track.

With much more room to operate, Martin won his fourth straight race, leading more than half the way while winning the Mountain Dew Southern 500 at Darlington Raceway in South Carolina. Martin described Darlington as a track "where you put on four tires when you stop, and you can pass so it shouldn't come down to fuel mileage. We've been going there for a long time and I've always enjoyed that type of racing."[3] Rain delayed and interrupted the race at Darlington, which was then cut sixteen laps short because of darkness.

Five years passed before any other NASCAR driver won four races in a row. Only seven have won four straight, and none have won five during the modern era, which NASCAR defines as beginning in 1972.

Martin had a shot at a longer streak. In the race right before his streak began, he finished third behind Dale Earnhardt and Ernie Irvan in the Die Hard 500 at Talladega in July.

With a chance to add a fifth straight win, Martin led 155 of the 400 laps at the Miller Genuine Draft 400 in Richmond in September. He remained on the lead lap but ultimately had to settle for sixth place.

Martin went into the streak a distant fifth in the season point standings and just missed climbing into second when it was done. The streak allowed him to comfortably settle into third place, a position he held when the season was finished.

RECORD CHALLENGE

Five years passed until Jeff Gordon not only matched the streak that Martin and five others produced, but also made a serious run at breaking the record.

Martin already had four wins in the 1998 season, but Gordon was even hotter. Gordon had eight and was on his way to thirteen while taking the points title. In the eight races coming into the Goody's 500 in Bristol, Gordon had been in the top three every time and had won four races in a row.

Martin, however, made sure that no one, including Gordon, had a chance in this race.

In the race he dedicated to his father and other family members who were killed in a private plane crash less than two weeks earlier, Martin took the lead on the 320th lap and held it for the final 181 laps of the race.

The win was just the second for Martin at Bristol, but both were significant—one for matching a series record and the other for protecting his share of the record.

Gordon was left to settle for fifth place. "The five in a row was cool to go for," said Gordon, who went on to win the next two races for six wins in seven tries. "I'm glad we won four in a row, but it's tough to do."[4]

Martin was one of the few drivers tough enough to do it.

DID YOU KNOW?

Jeff Gordon's incredible 1998 season overshadowed what may have been the best season of Mark Martin's career. Martin set a career high in 1998 with seven NASCAR Cup wins.

1998 NASCAR CUP STANDINGS

1.	Jeff Gordon	5,328
2.	Mark Martin	4,964
3.	Dale Jarrett	4,619
4.	Rusty Wallace	4,501
5.	Jeff Burton	4,415
6.	Bobby Labonte	4,180
7.	Jeremy Mayfield	4,157
8.	Dale Earnhardt	3,928
9.	Terry Labonte	3,901
10.	Bobby Hamilton	3,786

MR. VERSATILITY

Mark Martin has driven a stock car to victory on the tight, banked curves of the Bristol Motor Speedway, a track just over a half-mile in length. He has driven a truck to wins on superspeedways. He has taken the wheel of an IROC car, prepared identically to every other car in the field, and driven to wins on road courses. There was a time in the early days when Martin showed he could win racing on dirt.

Take any racing vehicle and any combination of surface and distance for a track, and chances are Martin has

Jeff Burton leads the pack, including Mark Martin (second row, left), to the finish line in the International Race of Champions on June 13, 1998.

some history of success. That history often includes wins and always seems to include consistency.

While ranking as one of the top drivers in the NASCAR Cup series, Martin never left NASCAR's Busch Series behind. He set records for the most wins in the Busch Series and for the most wins in the International Race of Champions, a series that brings top drivers from different types of racing together each year. Martin won four of the five IROC championships from 1994 to 1998.

As his career was beginning to wind down, Martin became a dominant force and a threat to win whenever he entered a NASCAR truck race. In his first seventeen starts, he won seven times.

CUP CONTENDER

There are two ways to measure Martin's NASCAR career. He is well aware that it is often pointed out that he did not finish any season as the sport's number-one driver. Martin is often in contention for the points championship, but he has had to settle for second place four times without ever winning.

The first and closest of those near misses in the points races came in 1990. Martin was penalized forty-six points for an early-season rules violation that team owner Jack Roush still disputes. Martin wound up losing the season points race by twenty-six points.

HOW THE NASCAR POINTS SYSTEM WORKS

NASCAR uses a points system, based primarily on the place finish in each race, to determine its overall champion each season.

The winner of each Cup race is awarded 180 points. The runner-up gets 170 points, and the points continue dropping from there. For example: fifth place earns 155, tenth place receives 134, twenty-first place receives 100, thirtieth place receives 73, on down to forty-third place, which receives 34 points.

A bonus of five points is issued to any driver who leads at the end of at least one lap during the race. The driver who leads the most laps in a race receives an additional five bonus points.

Points are accumulated throughout the first twenty-six races of the season. Drivers need to be in the top twelve at that point to be eligible to win the all-season championship in the Chase for the Nextel Cup. The drivers on that list have their point totals adjusted, making for a closer race heading into the stretch run of the season.

At the start of the Chase each of the twelve drivers has his point total adjusted to 5,000. They receive ten additional points for each race victory during the first part of the season. Then only those twelve drivers can earn points toward winning the overall Nextel Cup championship over the final 10 races of the season.

Martin won the Pontiac Excitement 400 at Richmond, but the dimensions of Martin's intake valve were called into question. Roush Racing claimed it followed a rules bulletin, which was issued by NASCAR after the rule book had been published. NASCAR determined that the rule in the book had been violated.

According to Jack Roush, NASCAR president Bill France said the bulletin and Roush's interpretation were not clear.

"But it was clear," Roush said. "It was clear to the technical people, it was clear to the competitors, it was clear to Mark, and it was clear to me that a deal had been made—an unholy deal had been made that cost us the championship."[1]

Jim Hunter, NASCAR vice president of corporate communications, disputes Roush's view of the ruling. "What happened to Roush Racing in 1990 was a clear rules violation," Hunter said. "I'm sure there were other instances during the season when Mark Martin had problems in other races. It didn't boil down to one event where the violation cost him the championship."[2]

Martin led in points with two races remaining in the season. Earnhardt moved in front by winning the Checker 500 at Phoenix while Martin was tenth. Earnhardt held on in the last race by finishing third in the Atlanta Journal 500, while Martin took sixth.

CLOSE CALLS
A look at Mark Martin's four second-place finishes in the NASCAR Cup points standings:

Year	Winner	Margin of Victory
1990	Dale Earnhardt	26 points
1994	Dale Earnhardt	444 points
1998	Jeff Gordon	364 points
2002	Tony Stewart	38 points

By every measure but a comparison with Earnhardt in the points race, 1990 was a wildly successful season for Martin. He won three races, finished in the top five sixteen times, and had twenty-three total finishes in the top ten.

Although he is frequently asked, Martin tries to avoid discussions about the points races and puts emphasis on other areas. "I used to worry myself to death about points," Martin said. "I refuse to do that. I'm going to go out and run every lap as hard as I can and try to win every race, and that's it. I'm never again going to sit around counting points."[3]

Martin wound up second again in 1994, 1998, and 2002 and placed third four times. Once he was connected with Roush Racing, Martin could be

MOST WINS IN NASCAR CUP MODERN ERA
(through end of 2006 season)

1.	Darrell Waltrip	84
2.	Dale Earnhardt	76
3.	Jeff Gordon	75
4.	Cale Yarborough	69
5.	Richard Petty	60
6.	Bobby Allison	55
6.	Rusty Wallace	55
8.	David Pearson	45
9.	Bill Elliott	44
10.	Mark Martin	35

counted on to be a contender and one of the sport's most successful drivers every season. His third-place finish in 1989 started a stretch of twelve straight seasons in which Martin was never ranked lower than eighth at the end of the year.

As of the end of the 2006 NASCAR season, Martin had earned the pole position forty-one times by leading qualifying. That total ranked sixth highest in the modern era of NASCAR Cup racing. In addition, he ranked tenth on the all-time victory list with thirty-five wins.

Mark Martin and his wife arrive at the Nextel Cup Series Awards ceremony on December 2, 2005, in New York.

BUSCH SERIES 25 GREATEST DRIVERS
(according to 2006 NASCAR.com fan poll)

1.   Mark Martin
2.   Dale Earnhardt, Jr.
3.   Kevin Harvick
4.   Dale Earnhardt
5.   Martin Truex Jr.
6.   Harry Gant
7.   Matt Kenseth
8.   Jeff Burton
9.   Bobby Labonte
10. Greg Biffle
11. Darrell Waltrip
12. Kenny Wallace
13. Joe Nemechek
14. Randy LaJoie
15. Dale Jarrett
16. Johnny Benson
17. Sam Ard
18. David Green
19. Michael Waltrip
20. Ron Hornaday Jr.
21. Jack Ingram
22. Jeff Green
23. Tommy Houston
24. Jimmy Spencer
25. Brian Vickers

Those numbers made it clear why Martin's name was included when NASCAR named its Greatest 50 Drivers as part of its fiftieth anniversary celebration in 1998.

RECORD-SETTING RACER

Martin used a full-time run on the Busch Series, NASCAR's second-highest level of racing, in 1987 as a springboard back to racing's big-time. Even as a regular contender in the Cup series, Martin never turned his back on the Busch Series.

In the 1988 and 1989 seasons, then again from 1992 through 1999, Martin ran about half of the Busch Series races each season. Martin took part in at least five races every season through 2000.

Martin did not just run races on the Busch Series. He ran them better than anyone in history. Martin won eleven of the twenty-five Busch races he entered at Rockingham and a total of forty-seven races in the series.

The forty-seven wins, as well as his thirty times earning the pole as the top qualifier, are both career records in Busch.

When the Busch Series celebrated its twenty-fifth season in 2006, it used two polls to name its 25 Greatest Drivers and rank them in order. One poll was an Internet poll for fans on NASCAR.com; the other was for media members.

BUSCH SERIES 25 GREATEST DRIVERS
(according to 2006 NASCARMedia.com media poll)

1.   Mark Martin
2.   Sam Ard
3.   Dale Earnhardt, Jr.
4.   Jack Ingram
5.   Dale Earnhardt
6.   Harry Gant
7.   Kevin Harvick
8.   Tommy Houston
9.   Randy LaJoie
10. Tommy Ellis
11. David Green
12. Greg Biffle
13. Jeff Green
14. Matt Kenseth
15. Bobby Labonte
16. Chuck Bown
17. Martin Truex Jr.
18. Jeff Burton
19. Larry Pearson
20. Jason Keller
21. Johnny Benson
22. Darrell Waltrip
23. Joe Nemechek
24. Rob Moroso
25. Dale Jarrett

Both groups came to the same conclusion: Mark Martin was the greatest driver in the first twenty-five years of the Busch Series. "I'd like to say thanks to both the fans and the media," Martin said. "We've always gone out and given 100 percent to whatever we were doing and to be recognized for our efforts means as much as any of the wins or any of the trophies."[4]

Martin won half of his fourteen starts in 1993, six out of fourteen in both 1996 and 1999, and six out of fifteen in 1997. "We had a lot of fun racing in the Busch Series," Martin said. "There has been a lot of talent in that series over the years, both with the full-time Cup guys and some of the Busch regulars, so to be voted at the top of the top 25 really does mean a lot to me."[5]

BEST OF THE BEST

The concept of the International Race of Champions (IROC) is to place the top drivers from each series—all-stars is one comparison that is often made—in equal

MARK MARTIN'S IROC WINS

1994	Darlington
1995	Darlington
1996	Charlotte
1996	Michigan
1997	Charlotte
1997	Fontana
1998	Fontana
1998	Indianapolis
1999	Indianapolis
2000	Indianapolis
2003	Daytona
2005	Daytona
2005	Richmond

cars and see who is the best. Rules are all designed to eliminate the advantage one crew can create and to make other team factors, such as pit stops, as insignificant as possible.

"Our first priority is to make sure that all the cars are equal," IROC president Jay Signore said. "Every part is the same. Each car is built exactly the same way. When the cars go on the track, they are as equal as it is humanly possible to make them."[6]

NASCAR drivers generally do very well when racing head to head with top foreign drivers as well as the best among Indy Car and Sprint Car drivers in the United States. None have done better than Martin.

In a series designed to determine the best of the best, Martin stands out as the most successful driver ever. "We don't know if IROC determines who the best driver in the world is, but we sure go a long way toward that goal," IROC chairman Les Richter said. "IROC does prove that some drivers have more skill than others regardless of their specialty or background."[7]

IROC, a four-race series spread over the year, has gotten together since 1973, inviting a small group of top drivers—usually a dozen. More than 100 drivers have been invited at least one time, but a small group has stood out.

Martin, in particular, put together some impressive credentials in the series:

Mark Martin celebrates a win in the 2006 GM FlexFuel 250 truck race in Daytona Beach, Florida.

- He won the series five times—1994, 1996, 1997, 1998, and 2005.
- He was the only driver to win one event three times in a row, taking the Indianapolis race in 1998, 1999, and 2000.
- He holds the record for winning the most races with thirteen.
- Although the series consists of just four races a season, Martin won at least one for the nine straight years that he was invited. In four of the seasons, he won twice.

"The success that I have had in IROC has meant more to me than anything else in my career," Martin said.[8]

Martin broke the record for most wins on February 18, 2005, with a victory at Daytona, his first of two on the season. Running in his tenth season of IROC, Martin broke the record for wins that he shared with Dale Earnhardt, who had been invited to the series a record seventeen times, and Al Unser Jr., who had been part of IROC fifteen times.

TRUCKING ALONG

The first time Martin ever tried a Craftsman Truck Series race was in 1996. He entered two races, finishing third in his debut and then winning the Lowe's 250 at North Wilkesboro Speedway in North Carolina.

Martin had established that he could drive a truck as well—or maybe even better—as a car, but he did not return to the series for more than nine years. He entered the Ford 200, the last of twenty-five races in the 2005 season, and finished eighth.

"It's been a long time since we ran a truck race, and I've really been itching to get back in that series, as that is where our future lies," Martin said. "We are going to run a handful of truck races next season as well and then go full time in '07, so this should be a good way to tell exactly where we are with the program."[9]

When Martin made the move to entering a little more than half the races in 2006, the results were immediate. He won six of his fourteen races, leading the series in victories despite his part-time status.

Martin gave an example of how dominant he can be in a truck on August 23, 2006, at Bristol. Martin won the pole and led 164 of the 200 laps, including the final 131 in which he was rarely challenged.

The only time any truck moved in front of Martin during the entire race was when he was making pit stops. Not once was he passed on the track. The win was the eighty-seventh in Martin's NASCAR career, counting Cup, Busch, and truck series races, moving him into fourth on the all-time list.

"We quit practice early, and the truck was spectacular," Martin said. "We had the truck that we needed to save tires and save gas 'til it came time to lower the hammer."[10]

The sight of Martin pulling away from them on every restart had to make the regulars in the truck series dread the prospect of Martin someday joining them full time. Martin, not quite ready to pull back entirely from Cup races, had to put on hold any ideas of driving truck series races full-time in 2007. He did make six starts in the truck series, and finished in the top five three times. His average finish was better than thirteenth place.

HOMETOWN HERO

There was a time, Mark Martin now admits, when he could not wait to leave Batesville.

As a Florida resident who travels the country to compete with other racecar drivers, Martin treasures his chances to return to Arkansas.

"Growing up, I couldn't wait to get out of Batesville and go and out and see what I could do," Martin said. "I went off seeking my fame and fortune, and I was fortunate to work with a lot of great people and have a lot of success. Now it's time to bring all of that back home where it belongs to Batesville."[1]

CARS ON DISPLAY AT MARK MARTIN MUSEUM

No. 6 Viagra car used to win Coca-Cola 600

1989 Stroh's Thunderbird

1990 Folgers Thunderbird

No. 60 Winn Dixie Busch car

2005 car used to win fifth IROC championship

To the people of Batesville, Martin is more than a racecar driver. A return home for a day to meet with his fans and sign autographs can bring out as many as 10,000 people. Martin is a hometown hero and a local businessman. Martin owns a car dealership in Batesville. The car dealership includes a museum highlighting Martin's career.

"It's just an awesome thing to be able to bring back all of these cars and trophies to the place where it all started and the place I consider home," Martin said while preparing for the museum opening in 2006.

Martin places his hands in cement as his wife, Elaine, and son Matt look on during a 2005 ceremony at Lowe's Motor Speedway.

TROPHIES AND MORE

The awards on display at the Mark Martin Museum in Batesville, Arkansas, help tell the story of Martin's career.

One example is the trophy from the 1993 Budweiser at the Glen race, a win that started Martin's career-best streak of four straight NASCAR Cup victories. A wire connects a lug nut to the trophy he was given that day.

"We made a pit stop and put three new tires on, and they couldn't change the right rear," Martin said. "We shouldn't have won that race. We struggled through the race. Ran that right rear through two stops, finally got it changed."

Robin Pemberton, who was changing the tire that day for Martin's crew, saved the lug nut and made it part of the trophy.

"We have a lot of stuff on display at the museum, and I hope that all of the fans will get a chance to come out and share in all of the memories with us."[2]

Several of Martin's cars are on display, along with other memorabilia and equipment. There are also some of Martin's personal photo albums, along with books of newspaper clippings chronicling Martin's career from its start on local dirt tracks through his career as a perennial NASCAR Cup contender.

"We really wanted to do something that we could share with the fans and the people of Batesville," Martin said.[3]

Before the museum, there was the car dealership that Martin also wanted to use to reconnect with his community. "We could have put the dealership anywhere," Martin said. "But I wanted to bring all of it home. It means a lot to me, and I'm excited to share what I've been lucky enough to experience with everyone."[4]

NEW HOME

Martin is raising his family in Daytona Beach, Florida. Although Daytona Beach is one of the most famous locations in auto racing, living there keeps Martin somewhat separated from the hustle and bustle that goes with life on the NASCAR circuit.

Much of the activity surrounding NASCAR is based in the Charlotte, North Carolina area, where many drivers live and many of the teams are based. "The distance between myself and the 'hub' is something that's really, really good for my family and me," Martin said. "The folks here in Daytona are different, and they treat me different than the mania of the Carolinas. We're sort of outside the mania and hysteria that goes along with the sport."[5]

STARTING ANOTHER CAREER

From his home in Florida, Martin is able to repeat a scenario he lived out as a

MARK MARTIN'S FAMILY

Wife: **Arlene**

Children: **Amy, Rachel, Heather, Stacy, Matt**

Martin and his son Matt introduce a new comic book, Race Warrior, at a news conference in 2000.

youngster. Mark's son, Matt, is now learning how to race cars and trucks. At fourteen, the same age Mark was when he began racing, Matt already had quite a bit of experience. As an eight-year-old in 1999, Matt won the season championship in the Junior Novice Division of the Mid-Florida Quarter Midget Association. Matt moved up in class the next year, and his father was there to see his first win on a higher level.

"I was glad my Dad was there when I won," Matt said. "When he's not there, we always call him after my races to tell him how I did in each one."[6]

Before he was eligible to apply for a driver's license, Matt was racing against grown men in the pro truck and fast truck series in Florida. Matt's home track as a Limited Late Model series driver in 2006, the New Smyrna Speedway, was the site of one of Mark's first big races on pavement as he graduated from dirt tracks.

Matt splits his time between trying to develop his own career and following what may be the later stages of Mark's career. "We usually run at least once a month, sometimes two," Matt said. "I can't really race all the time because I'm always with Dad at the track."[7]

Mark is trying to teach Matt to control his aggressiveness and be a patient racecar driver. To aid in that process, the NASCAR star avoids the temptation to always put his son in the best possible car.

"He doesn't need a great car to learn," Mark said.[8]

DID YOU KNOW?

Quarter Midgets are miniature racecars designed for drivers five to sixteen years old. The cars offer young people the opportunity to learn how to race. Quarter Midgets are broken down into fifteen classes. The cars have one-cylinder engines that produce between 2.5 and 4 horsepower.

Matt, of course, would like to see how he could do in a great car. "He knows more about a racecar than most other people," Matt said. "I have the driver's suit and shoes on, but he's really in control."[9]

Despite any discussions they might have, Mark said his son is listening—and learning. "He doesn't agree with me," Mark said. "He thinks he's going to win no matter what. But I tell him what we're going to do, and he listens."[10]

With Matt now driving a Ford with 480 horsepower, the experience can be tough on parents. "I got so nervous," Arlene Martin, Mark's wife, admits.[11] Mark also admits the nerves are there. "I'm just like any other dad. I want what's best for my kid. I could be doing the same thing if he was getting ready for a football game. I just wouldn't know what to tell him."[12]

Matt says he wants to do more than just share a sport with his father. He would like to someday develop the reputation Mark has as one of the sport's true gentlemen.

"It makes me real happy and proud that people think he's a nice person and someone who's fair to people," Matt said. "I hope when I get older, I act like him."[13]

Martin celebrates a win with his son, Matt, after the wreck-filled UAW-GM 500 in 1998.

TOUGH TO SAY GOODBYE

The message from Mark Martin in the 2005 season was supposed to be "so long." Martin and his public relations team even put a title on the season, calling it the "Salute to You" tour.

By the time 2005 was done, however, Martin and team owner Jack Roush had a different message: "not so fast." A fourth-place finish in the overall NASCAR Cup point standings was just one of the reasons that decisions were made determining that it was not yet time for Martin to retire from stock car racing's highest division. The salute was planned to honor everyone that Martin thought had played a big role in his career. The fans who supported him were a big part of the salute.

SENDING A SALUTE

Early in the racing season, Martin was home in Arkansas to meet with those fans. The Salute to You Fans Day was held at Martin's Ford-Mercury dealership in Batesville on the last weekend of March. Martin brought in reigning NASCAR Cup champion Kurt Busch and long-time rival Rusty Wallace for a day each to sign autographs for fans.

"We are excited about fan day," Martin said. "It's part of our 'Salute to You' Tour, and we are hoping to get out and meet a lot of fans in the course of the two days. In addition, I've called in some favors, and we have our Nextel Cup champion Kurt Busch coming in. . . . We also have my long-time racing friend and rival Rusty Wallace. . . . Rusty and I go back a long, long way, and it really means a lot to me for him to take one of his few off days of a busy season and come here and do this for me."[1]

Batesville was where it all started for Martin, so why not use it as the starting point for what, at the time, he thought was going to be the wrap-up to his career. "That's what this year is all about. We want to get out and meet as many people as we can and be

able to let them all know just how much their support has meant to us. I can't think of a better way to do that or a better place to start," he said.[2]

As it turned out, Martin came up with an even better way to celebrate his career—by showing he could still succeed, and that, at age forty-six, he still had a future behind the wheel.

The "Salute to You" theme was never abandoned, but as the season progressed, it turned into a different type of celebration. While celebrating past relationships and memories, Martin still had chances to enjoy current success.

Martin saluted crowds throughout a competitive but unspectacular first two-thirds of the 2005 season. He finished in the top ten in four of the first six races, then twice put together streaks of three straight top-ten finishes.

Martin appeared to be picking up some momentum when he finished seventh in New Hampshire and fourth in Delaware, but a crash knocked him out in Lap 19 at Talladega, leaving him in forty-first place out of the forty-three cars that started the race.

A SPECIAL DAY

When Martin arrived at Kansas Speedway in Kansas City, Kansas, the morning of October 19, 2005, he was

Martin is honored before the start of the Dodge Charger 500 at Darlington Speedway on May 7, 2005.

sitting in ninth place in the NASCAR Cup standings. By the end of the day, he was sitting behind the wheel of a winning car for the first time all season.

Martin went to the starting line in nineteenth position for the Banquet 400, but he moved up through the pack and assumed control of the race. He wound up leading for all but one lap of the second half of the race.

Crew chief Pat Tryson made the decision to change two tires at a time in pit stops to gain ground on the field. The first time, during a caution on Lap 17, allowed Martin to jump all the way from fourteenth place to third. The second time, in Lap 121, Martin went from tenth place into the lead.

Except for brief cycles when he took his pit stop before an opponent, Martin led the rest of the race. Tony Stewart was lined up next to Martin on restarts following cautions twice late in the race, but Martin pulled away both times.

"It's a really special day for me," Martin said in Victory Lane. "I want to thank all the fans for the great support I've had this year. . . . This Ford was incredible today. It reminded me of the old days in a Busch car. It was just awesome. These guys want to win so badly, and they believe in me, and they made a winner out of this old man today."[3]

Martin led for more than half of the laps and held off teammate Greg Biffle in the end to win

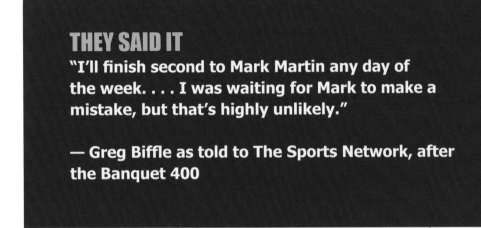

THEY SAID IT
"I'll finish second to Mark Martin any day of the week. . . . I was waiting for Mark to make a mistake, but that's highly unlikely."

— Greg Biffle as told to The Sports Network, after the Banquet 400

by a little more than half a second. Another Roush driver, Carl Edwards, followed to give the team a 1-2-3 finish.

"It was almost a relief to cross that finish line," Martin said. "I had a lot of laps out front to worry about what could go wrong. I thought I could hold off Tony, but when I saw Biffle get by him pretty easy, I knew I'd have to drive the fool out of the thing like he does to stay in front. I didn't want to lose and we did what we had to in order to get this win."[4]

A LATE CLIMB

The win turned out to be the only one of the season for Martin, but it sparked a strong finish that sent him climbing through the points standings. Counting the win in Kansas, Martin finished in the top five in five of the last seven races. He had a third- and two

BIG FINISH
Mark Martin's last seven race results in 2005

Date	Race	Site	Start	Finish
10/9	Banquet 400	Kansas	19	1
10/15	UAW-GM Quality 500	Charlotte	6	5
10/23	Subway 500	Martinsville	35	34
10/30	Bass Pro Shop MBNA 500	Atlanta	4	3
11/6	Dickies 500	Fort Worth	8	2
11/13	Checkers Auto Parts 500	Phoenix	29	14
11/20	Ford 400	Homestead	5	2

second-place finishes in the last four races of the year. Carl Edwards beat Martin by a little more than half a second, and Matt Kenseth came in third during another 1-2-3 finish for Roush Racing at the Dickies 500 in Texas to begin November.

There was a time when November 20, 2005, was planned as the end of the full-time portion of Martin's racing career. Before the Ford 400 started at Homestead-Miami Speedway, there were many indications that the plan would be changing.

Martin showed why the message at the end of the 2005 season was much different than the one he and his team had been expressing at the start. Starting the race from the fifth position, Martin did not feel comfortable with the car early and slipped back to twelfth by the ninth lap. The feel improved and so did Martin's position in the race. He was in the top ten for good by Lap 34 of the 267-lap race.

Martin led the race briefly as the top cars went through a series of pit stops, and he ran second for much of the latter part of the race. The Roush Racing team as a whole, and Martin in particular, came racing to the final finish line in style.

Coming out of Turn 4, Martin cut to the inside and was able to pull up alongside Biffle. Biffle beat a hard-charging Martin by inches, finishing just .017 seconds (about 1/60th of a second) in front. They combined with Kenseth and Edwards on a sweep of the top four spots for Roush.

"That was a great race," Martin said. "Man, was it close. I thought we were going to be able to pull it off, but we were just inches short."[5]

The man who had been planning retirement clearly had the fire to keep competing. "I guess maybe we needed another lap, or maybe I would have crashed trying," Martin said.

"I raced Greg hard, and I raced him clean and vice versa, and he was in front when it was over. I would have loved to have won, but I guess only one guy can win. We had a great run, a great finish, and a great year, and we were able to move up to fourth in the points in the last race."[6]

Winning the All-Star Challenge was only one reason why Martin had the time of his life in 2005. He earned $1.1 million for winning the race.

2005 NASCAR NEXTEL CUP POINTS STANDINGS

1.	Tony Stewart	6,533
2. (tied)	Greg Biffle	6,498
2. (tied)	Carl Edwards	6,498
4.	Mark Martin	6,428
5.	Jimmie Johnson	6,406
6.	Ryan Newman	6,359
7.	Matt Kenseth	6,352
8.	Rusty Wallace	6,140
9.	Jeremy Mayfield	6,073
10.	Kurt Busch	5,974

When it was done, Martin said, "I've had the time of my life in 2005."[7] That made it tough for him to avoid thinking about 2006 and beyond. "I hope we can keep these guys together for another year, and we'll come back and make one more run at this thing."[8]

Jack Roush was thinking the same thing. When Roush ran into complications negotiating with drivers for his 2006 teams, he asked Martin to return to drive one more year. A deal was reached in October to

Martin checks his tires during practice for the 2005 Bass Pro Shops MBNA 500.

have Martin return to his No. 6 car, which would go through a change in major sponsorship to AAA.

Martin and Roush agreed on a revised plan that had Martin entering 2006 again planning for what would be a final NASCAR Cup series before moving into the somewhat less-demanding NASCAR Craftsman Truck series for future years. In preparation for the move, Martin returned to the truck series for the last race of 2005 and fourteen races in 2006.

STILL COMPETITIVE

When he ended up fourth in the final NASCAR Cup points standings in 2005, Martin had his third top-five overall finish in the last four years. Clearly, his performance did not dictate the need to retire.

Martin started 2006 the same way. Thirteen races into the 2006 season, he was in third place in the overall standings. It seemed like time to once again re-evaluate the future.

Martin holds the trophy after winning the Stater Brothers 300 on February 26, 2005.

10

MAKING CHANGES

Slowing down in what is supposed to be the final year on the job might make sense to some people. It runs against the concept of racing, however.

Mark Martin entered 2006 thinking for the second time that it might be his last season before semi-retirement. All Martin did was plan a schedule that was busier than ever and combined new challenges with the accustomed grind of a season in the NASCAR Cup series.

Martin ran every Cup race, increased his test of the Craftsman

Martin leads the pack of trucks to the green flag at the start of the GM FlexFuel 250 on February 17, 2006.

Truck Series, and continued running in some Busch Series races and all four IROC events. "Last year, I was preparing myself for my last year in Cup, and there was a lot of emotion and a lot of things going on that I was focused on," Martin said. "This year, I'm just trying to keep afloat. I'm treading water."[1]

Martin deflected questions of whether the schedule might make him too busy. "I haven't thought about it, and I don't know if I'm going to think about it," he said. "I don't really have a philosophy."[2]

There was enough for Martin to think about. The veteran split the truck season schedule with David Ragan, adding a new twist to his career, serving as mentor for a younger driver who not only worked as a teammate but in driving the same vehicle.

The truck series turned out to be a perfect fit for Martin. He won the first two races of the series in February at Daytona and at California

Martin celebrates his win in the 2006 GM FlexFuel 250.

Speedway in Fontana. "Man, I'm having a blast," Martin said after his second straight win.[3]

Martin slowed down slightly after the two wins, slipping to second and fourth in his next two races. After only running three previous truck races, Martin entered fourteen of the twenty races in 2006, winning six times and finishing in the top five eleven times.

"The truck racing is the most fun I've had in years and years," Martin said.[4]

Nobody else won as often as Martin even though he was just a part-timer. He finished nineteenth in points, but seventeen of the eighteen drivers above him entered all twenty-five races and the other was in twenty-four.

Along the way, Martin thoroughly enjoyed a new experience in racing. "We've just had a lot of fun going out and competing in truck races," Martin said. "In my opinion, it's the best racing in NASCAR, and I'm glad to get to be a part of it. It's the least spoiled by commercialism. It feels very pure."[5]

MARK MARTIN'S TRUCK SERIES WINS

Date	Race	Site
September 28, 1996	Lowe's 250	North Wilkesboro
February 17, 2006	GM Flex Fuel 250	Daytona
February 24, 2006	racetickets.com 200	Fontana
June 2, 2006	AAA Insurance 200	Dover
August 23, 2006	O'Reilly Auto Parts 200	Bristol
October 7, 2006	John Deere 250	Talladega
November 17, 2006	Ford 200	Homestead

Martin kept producing in the NASCAR Cup series as well. Through the middle part of the season, he finished in the top five at New Hampshire, Indianapolis, Michigan, Richmond, and Kansas. Those finishes came during a span of eleven races in which he moved up from his starting position eight times and matched it another time. Although he was not qualifying among the top drivers, he was racing well enough to qualify as one of the ten drivers in the Chase for the Nextel Cup for the points championship.

The success created a new variation of an old dilemma. A year earlier, Martin was ready to step aside, but the Roush Racing team needed him. This time, the Roush Racing team was preparing a plan for Martin to race trucks in 2007, but Martin had decided he still wanted to be part of the Cup series.

Complicated negotiations ensued involving many teams and drivers. When the negotiations were done, the nineteen-year working relationship between Martin and Jack Roush came to an end. Roush Racing president Geoff Smith said his team did not have a spot available in the Cup series, and Martin wound up landing a deal to run about twenty races for MB2, switching from his famous seat in the No. 6 car to the No. 01 U.S. Army car.

"When you can compete like I have been the last couple of years in this type of competition, it's hard to step away from it," Martin said.[6]

CONSISTENTLY IN THE CHASE

NASCAR started a new points format prior to the 2004 season in an effort to inject more excitement into the final weeks of the season each year.

Starting in 2004, only the top ten drivers (and any others within 400 points of the lead), competed for the overall season championship. This added pressure and excitement to the first twenty-six races of the season, as drivers attempted to accumulate points in order to qualify for the season-ending "Chase for the Cup."

After twenty-six races, the top ten was determined, and only those racers accumulated points over the remaining ten weeks of the season. To make it even more exciting, this top ten had their point totals reset, so they were all certain to be within reach of the lead. This way, they would each have a chance to win the overall season championship.

Through the first three years of this new format, only three drivers had qualified in the top ten in all three years—Mark Martin, Matt Kenseth, and Jimmie Johnson.

CHANGES ANNOUNCED

Martin's change in plans for the 2007 season was announced on October 6 with six races still remaining in the 2006 season. MB2 Motorsports announced that Martin would co-drive the No. 01 car with rookie Regan Smith for the 2007 season.

"Our goal at MB2 is to reach a new level, and with Mark joining our organization it not only elevates

Martin talks to his crew members in the garage area before practice at the Daytona 500.

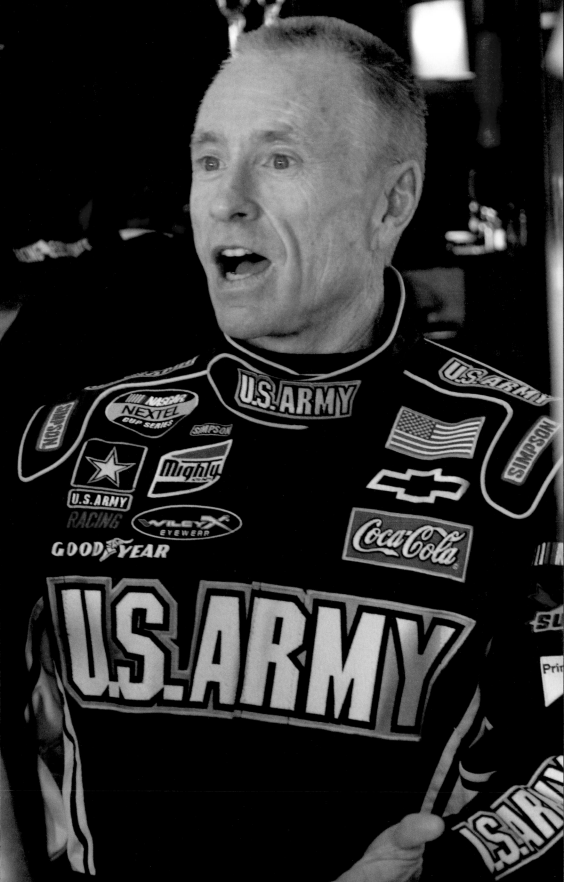

THEY SAID IT
"Mark Martin is one of NASCAR's greatest competitors and having him come on board will greatly enhance and accelerate our development."

— Jay Frye, MB2 CEO and general manager

our presence, but his knowledge and credibility will also be a viable asset to all our race teams," team owner Bobby Ginn said.[7]

Ginn pointed out that it was an advantage to the team to have Regan "groomed" by one of the greatest drivers in NASCAR history. "Joining MB2 is a win-win situation for me," Martin said. "I not only get to drive, but I also get to teach, and I love doing both. I've had a great 19 years with Roush Racing. It was a difficult decision to move on."[8]

Martin's long and comfortable working relationship with Roush made for a shocking announcement. "I've had a strong relationship with Mark ever since joining Ford racing, and I speak for everyone at Ford when I say that Mark has earned the right to do whatever he wants as far as his racing career is concerned," Ford Racing Technology director Dan Davis said. "He's been the ultimate competitor on the

Martin waves the checkered flag from his car after winning the 2005 Nextel All-Star Challenge.

track and a great representative for Ford over the past two decades. That being said, I'm disappointed that Mark may not end his NASCAR career with Ford. We were under the strong impression that Mark wanted to run a full-time NASCAR Craftsman Truck Series program in 2007 and were negotiating with Roush Racing to provide manufacturer support."[9]

FINISHING THE SEASON

Martin still planned to continue his transition into truck racing, but MB2 provided him the opportunity to do that without giving up on the NASCAR Cup

Martin gets some final instructions from his crew as he prepares for a practice session.

2006 NASCAR CUP POINTS STANDINGS

1.	Jimmie Johnson	6,475
2.	Matt Kenseth	6,419
3.	Denny Hamlin	6,407
4.	Kevin Harvick	6,397
5.	Dale Earnhardt, Jr.	6,328
6.	Jeff Gordon	6,256
7.	Jeff Burton	6,228
8.	Kasey Kahne	6,183
9.	Mark Martin	6,168
10.	Kyle Busch	6,027

series. With the long-term future addressed, the final six weeks of racing with Roush still were ahead.

Two successful time trials in which he qualified seventh at Charlotte and Atlanta were wasted when he crashed late in each race. Martin put things together one more time in his closing run with his No. 6 car. He led twenty-six laps on the way to a sixth-place finish in the Checker Auto Parts 500 at Phoenix International Raceway in the next-to-last race of the season.

"It was awesome on long runs, and we didn't get much of that in the second half, but in the first half we were really mowing them down," Martin said of the climb from a twenty-first spot in qualifying. "I'm really proud of this team and proud of our run. We could hold our own against those guys once everything settled in, and we might have even done a little better with more green flag, but it was a great team effort."[10]

The season ended at Homestead a week later when Martin finished eighteenth at the Ford 400. Although the season did not quite match the lofty standards of earlier efforts by Martin, he did finish ninth in the final points standings during a time when he once figured to be in retirement.

"I'm very proud of the effort that has been made by Roush Racing and especially by the 6 team

HE SAID IT

"I was 39 years old when I started making plans for the future. I realize at this time that was way too early. I thought that, at this age, I wouldn't be able to compete with these young guys at this level."

— Mark Martin

Kevin Harvick (left) edges out Mark Martin to win the Daytona 500 in 2007.

all three years," Martin said. "The last three years have been phenomenal. We won't finish as high in the points this year as we did the other two years, so on paper it may not look as good, but believe me, the effort was spectacular."[11]

A NEW START

With Ginn's cooperation, Martin was able to scale back on his racing schedule in 2007. But the talent was still there. Martin opened the season by finishing second to Kevin Harvick in the Daytona 500. In one of the most memorable finishes in the history of the race, Martin lost by just two one-hundredths of a second.

After four races, Martin held the top spot in the Nextel Cup points standings. Many thought Martin might change his plans and resume full-time racing. But on March 25 at the Food City 500 at Bristol (Tenn.) Motor Speedway, Martin was not in the lineup, and his streak of 621 consecutive starts had come to an end. He was sticking to his plan, and spending more time with family. On that particular day, he was helping his son, Matt, prepare a car for a late model race.

Exactly where he said he would be.

Martin waits to qualify at New Hampshire International Speedway on September 15, 2006.

CAREER STATISTICS

Year	Rank	Starts	Wins	Poles
2007	27	24	0	0
2006	9	36	0	0
2005	4	36	1	0
2004	4	36	1	0
2003	17	36	0	0
2002	2	36	1	0
2001	12	36	0	2
2000	8	34	1	0
1999	3	34	2	1
1998	2	33	7	3
1997	3	32	4	3
1996	5	31	0	4
1995	4	31	4	4

Top 5	Top 10	Earnings	Points
5	11	$4,097,200	2,960
7	15	$4,282,550	6,168
12	19	$5,994,350	6,428
10	15	$3,948,500	6,399
5	10	$4,048,850	3,769
12	22	$5,279,400	4,762
3	15	$3,487,720	4,095
13	20	$2,763,540	4,410
19	26	$2,783,296	4,943
22	26	$3,279,370	4,964
16	24	$1,877,139	4,681
14	23	$1,887,396	4,278
13	22	$1,499,470	4,320

CAREER STATISTICS

Year	Rank	Starts	Wins	Poles
1994	2	31	2	1
1993	3	30	5	5
1992	6	29	2	1
1991	6	29	1	5
1990	2	29	3	3
1989	3	29	1	6
1988	15	29	0	1
1987	102	1	0	0
1986	48	5	0	0
1983	30	16	0	0
1982	14	30	0	0
1981	42	5	0	2

Top 5	Top 10	Earnings	Points
15	20	$1,054,240	4,250
12	19	$1,151,890	4,150
10	17	$807,505	3,887
14	17	$805,105	3,914
16	23	$803,095	4,404
14	18	$622,788	4,053
3	10	$189,400	3,142
0	0	$3,550	46
0	0	$20,515	364
1	3	$99,655	1,621
2	8	$115,600	3,042
1	2	$13,950	615

CAREER ACHIEVEMENTS

1977	American Speed Association (ASA) Rookie of the Year.
1978-1980	Won three straight ASA season championships.
1981	Won NASCAR Cup pole position for first time.
1986	Won ASA season championship.
1989	Won first career NASCAR Cup race at North Carolina Motor Speedway.
1990	Finished second in final NASCAR Cup points race.
1993	Won four straight NASCAR Winston Cup races.

1994	Won International Race of Champions (IROC) title; Finished second in final NASCAR Cup points race.
1993-1995	Became first NASCAR driver to win three straight races on road course at Watkins Glen.
1996-1998	Won three straight IROC titles.
1998	Won a career-high seven NASCAR Cup races to finish second in final points race.
2002	Finished second in NASCAR Cup points race.
2005	Set IROC record with twelfth career win.
2005	Won IROC title.

CHAPTER NOTES

CHAPTER 1. STILL GOING STRONG

1. "Roush Speaks on Martin's 600 Starts," *Nextel Cup News*, July 9, 2006. <http://www.stockcarreview.com/2006.07.09_arch.html> (November 17, 2006).
2. Ibid.
3. Mark Ashenfelter, "Martin is The Man," *The Scene blog*, July 16, 2006 http://blog.scenedaily.com/index.php/2006/07/page/5/ (November 17, 2006).
4. Michael Vega and Fluto Shinzawa, "Hamlin couldn't go the extra miles," *The Boston Globe*, July 17, 2006, http://www.boston.com/sports/articles/2006/07/17/hamlin_couldnt_go_the_extra_miles/ (November 17, 2006).
5. Mark Ashenfelter, "Martin is The Man," *The Scene blog*, July 16, 2006 http://blog.scenedaily.com/index.php/2006/07/page/5/ (November 17, 2006).
6. "Martin to Make Milestone 600th Consecutive Cup Start This Weekend," *Roush Racing Web site*, July 11, 2006, http://www.roushracing.com/mark_martin/articles/ab071106_276.htm.
7. Ibid.

CHAPTER 2. A DIRTY JOB

1. Bob Zeller, *Mark Martin—Driven to Drive*, Phoenix: David Bell Publishing, 1987, as cited in Tony Fabrizio, "Martin owes racing to late father," Augusta Chronicle, August 13, 1998, http://chronicle.august.com/stories/081398/spo_124-7668.shtml (December 28, 2006).
2. David Poole, "Martin ends Gordon's chase for record 5 straight wins," *The Charlotte Observer*, March 16, 2002, http://thatsracin.com/mld/thatsracin/archives/2873962.htm (January 3, 2007).
3. Tony Fabrizio, "Martin owes racing to late father," *Augusta Chronicle*, August 13, 1998, http://chronicle.august.com/stories/081398/spo_124-7668.shtml (December 28, 2006).

CHAPTER 3. MOVING UP

1. Lee Spencer, "Gold standard," *The Sporting News*, June 2, 2006, http://archive.sportingnews.com/exclusives/20060602/744065.html (December 29, 2006).
2. Ibid.

CHAPTER 4. GETTING STARTED

1. Lee Spencer, "Gold standard," *The Sporting News*, June 2, 2006, http://archive.sportingnews.com/exclusives/20060602/744065.html (December 29, 2006).

2. Larry Cothren, "Racing's Steady, Consistent And Complex Superstar," http://www.stockcarracing.com/thehistoryof/83738_mark_ martin (January 4, 2007).

3. Lee Spencer, "Gold standard," *The Sporting News*, June 2, 2006, http://archive.sportingnews.com/exclusives/20060602/744065.html (December 29, 2006).

CHAPTER 5. TEAM SPORT

1. Larry Cothren, "Racing's Steady, Consistent And Complex Superstar," http://www.stockcarracing.com/thehistoryof/83738_mark_ martin (January 4, 2007).

2. Larry Woody, "'My career is not in crisis': Mark Martin is arguably the greatest NASCAR driver never to win a Winston Cup championship—just don't remind him of that," *Auto Racing Digest*, June-July, 2003, <findarticles.com/p/articles/mi_m0FCH/is_4_31/ai_100046286> (January 10, 2007).

3. "Martin Enjoying Truck Series Success," *TruckSeries.com*, June 13, 2006, http://www.truckseries.com/cgi-script/NCTS_06/ articles/000074/007408.htm (January 10, 2007).

4. Dave Rodman, "Martin leaves door open for return to Roush," *NASCAR.com*, November 18, 2006, http://www.nascar.com/2006/news/ headlines/cup/11/18/mmartin_finale/index.html (January 4, 2007).

5. Ibid.

6. Ibid.

CHAPTER 6. WINNING STREAK

1. Kevin Woods, "Mark Martin Fast Facts—Food City 500," *Roush Racing*, March 28, 2005, <http://www.whowon.com/RF_Results.asp?Tra ckID=479&StoryID=145961> (January 3, 2007).

2. B. Duane Cross, "Wallace's success also has its disappointments," *NASCAR.com*, April 13, 2005, http://aol.nascar.com/2005/news/headlines/ cup/04/13/rwallace.oh.so.close/index.html (January 3, 2007).

3. "2003 Southern 500 Roush On Track," August 31, 2003, http://www.roushracing.com/lets_go_racing/articles/xg082703_017.htm (January 10, 2007).

4. David Poole, "Martin ends Gordon's chase for record 5 straight wins," *The Charlotte Observer*, March 16, 2002, http://thatsracin.com/mld/thatsracin/archives/2873962.htm (January 3, 2007).

CHAPTER 7. MR. VERSATILITY

1. Stephen Thomas, "Mark Martin: King Without A Crown," *The Sporting News*, October 10, 2002, http://www.angelfire.com/pa4/MarkMartinM6M/2002MarkMartinArticlesPage1.html (January 8, 2007).

2. Ibid.

3. Larry Woody, "'My career is not in crisis': Mark Martin is arguably the greatest NASCAR driver never to win a Winston Cup championship—just don't remind him of that," *Auto Racing Digest*, June-July, 2003, <findarticles.com/p/articles/mi_m0FCH/is_4_31/ai_100046286> (January 10, 2007).

4. "Martin wins Busch title – as series' greatest driver," *NASCAR.com,* November 15, 2006, http://www.nascar.com/2006/news/headlines/bg/11/15/busch.greatest.results/index.html (January 10, 2007).

5. Ibid.

6. "Series," http://www.irocracing.com/current_season/series.html (January 8, 2007).

7. Ibid.

8. Ibid.

9. "Martin Makes Return to Truck Series," November 18, 2005, http://www.roushracing.com/mark_martin/archive.asp?yr=2005 (January 10, 2007).

10. "Martin Dominates Bristol Truck Race; Becomes Fourth Winningest Driver in NASCAR History," August 23, 2006, http://www.roushracing.com/mark_martin/archive.asp?yr=2006 (January 10, 2007).

CHAPTER 8. HOMETOWN HERO

1. "Mark Martin Museum Grand Opening/Fan Days Set for This Weekend in Batesville," April 12, 2006, http://www.roushracing.com/mark_martin/archive.asp?yr=2006 (January 10, 2007).

2. Ibid.

3. Ibid.

4.   Ibid.

5.   Larry Cothren, "Racing's Steady, Consistent And Complex Superstar," http://www.stockcarracing.com/thehistoryof/83738_mark_ martin (January 4, 2007).

6.   "Matt Martin is off to a strong start," May 12, 2000, http://www. markmartin.org/mattmartin.html (January 5, 2007).

7.   David Newton, "Busy Martin still teaching son the family business," *NASCAR.com*, April 16, 2006, http://www.nascar.com/2006/ news/headlines/cup/04/16/mmartin_son/index.html (January 5, 2007).

8.   Ibid.

9.   Ibid.

10. Ibid.

11. Ibid.

12. Ibid.

13. Krista Voda, "Behind the Chase: Matt Martin follows father's tire tracks," *FOXSports.com*, October 24, 2005, http://msn.foxsports.com/ nascar/story/4992344 (January 5, 2007).

CHAPTER 9. TOUGH TO SAY GOODBYE

1.   "Mark Martin 'Salute to You' Fan Days Planned for Batesville on March 25 and 26," March 17, 2005, http://www.roushracing.com/mark_ martin/archive.asp?yr=2005 (January 10, 2007).

2.   Ibid.

3.   "Martin Posts Dominating Performance in Kansas Victory," October 10, 2005, http://www.roushracing.com/mark_martin/archive. asp?yr=2005 (January 10, 2007).

4.   Ibid.

5.   "Martin, Biffle Go Down to the Wire at Homestead Season Finale," November 21, 2005, http://www.roushracing.com/mark_martin/ archive.asp?yr=2005 (January 10, 2007).

6.   Ibid.

7.   Ibid.

8.   Ibid.

CHAPTER 10. MAKING CHANGES

1.   Rea White, "Martin plowing on," scenedaily.com, March 2, 2006, http://www.scenedaily.com/stories/2006/02/27/scene_daily192.html (January 10, 2007).

2. Ibid.

3. Jeff Wolf, "Martin hangs on for Craftsman victory," *Las Vegas Review-Journal*, February 25, 2006, <http://www.reviewjournal.com/lvrj_home/2006/Feb-25-Sat-2006/sports/6075571.html> (January 8, 2007).

4. "Martin Enjoying Truck Series Success," *TruckSeries.com*, June 13, 2006, http://www.truckseries.com/cgi-script/NCTS_06/articles/000074/007408.htm (January 8, 2007).

5. Ibid.

6. Tommy Thompson, "Mark Martin Finds Part-Time Work Away From Roush...And It's OK," October 11, 2006, http://www.frontstretch.com/tthompson/5600 (January 8, 2007).

7. "Mark Martin Enlists in the MB2 Army for 2007," October 6, 2006, http://www.fastmachines.com/archives/nascar/003971.php (January 7, 2007).

8. Ibid.

9. Ibid.

10. "Martin, No. 6 AAA Team Fight to Scrappy 6th-Place Finish," November 14, 2006, http://www.roushracing.com/mark_martin/archive.asp?yr=2005 (January 7, 2007).

11. "Martin Captures Ford 200 Truck Race," November 17, 2006, http://www.theautochannel.com/news/2006/11/17/029056.html (January 7, 2007).

FOR MORE INFORMATION

WEB LINKS

Martin's site from Roush, his long-time racing team:
http://www.roushracing.com/mark_martin/

Ginn Racing, Martin's new team:
http://www.ginnracing.com/

A fan site dedicated to Martin's career:
http://www.markmartin.org

Martin's page on the statistical racing source:
http://www.racing-reference.info/driver?id=martima01

FURTHER READING

Boone, Jerry F. Mark Martin: *The Racer's Racer.* St. Paul, Minn.: Motorbooks, 2006.

Martin, Mark and Beth Tuschak. *NASCAR for Dummies.* Hoboken, N.J.: Wiley, 2005.

Zeller, Bob. *Mark Martin: Driven to Race.* Phoenix: David Bell Publishing, 1997.

GLOSSARY

American Speed Association—A national touring series that sanctioned late model races, based in the Midwest.

banked—A sloped racetrack, usually at a curve or corner.

crew chief—The leader of the pit crew.

drafting—The aerodynamic effect that allows two or more cars traveling nose to tail to run faster than a car running by itself. The lead car cuts through the air, providing less resistance for the back car or cars.

groove—The best route around a racetrack.

intake valve—A valve in a car's engine that opens to allow the fuel/air mixture to enter the combustion chamber.

IROC car—A type of car that is prepared identically to every other car in the race field, so that driver skill is emphasized over pit crew skill.

lug nut—a large, cone-shaped piece of steel or metal that screws onto a bolt that is attached to a wheel.

pinch hitter—Due to a lack of sponsorship, a driver who races various makes of cars for various owners in a given season.

pit crew—The mechanics who work as a team to make adjustments to the car, such as changing tires, during a race.

pit road—The area where pit crews service the cars, usually along the front straightaway.

pole position—The leading position at the start of a race, awarded to the fastest driver during qualifying.

qualifying—A process where cars are timed in laps on the track by themselves. The times are then compared, with the fastest cars getting to start in the best positions for a race.

short track—A racetrack that is less than one mile long.

sponsor—A business that pays money to a race team, generally in exchange for advertising, such as having its logo painted on the car.

stock car—A standard type of automobile that is modified for use in racing.

superspeedway—A racetrack that is two miles or longer.

V-8 engine—An internal combustion engine with eight cylinders, found commonly in sports cars, sport utility vehicles and pickup trucks. The alignment of the cylinders on the crankshaft is shaped like a "V."

Victory Lane—The winner's circle where the winning driver parks to celebrate after the race.

INDEX

A

Allison, Bobby, 23, 31, 62
AAA, 93
American Speed Association (ASA), 12, 23-27, 34-37
Anderson Speedway, 24, 35
Atlanta Journal 500, 60

B

Banquet 400, 43, 84, 85, 86
Benton Speedbowl, 14
Biffle, Greg, 64, 65, 84, 85, 87, 90
Bristol, 17, 49, 50, 52, 54, 70, 98
Buckeye 400, 24
Bud at the Glen, 16, 74
Busch, Kurt, 81, 90
Busch Nashville 420, 30

C

California Speedway, 97
Chase for the Nextel Cup, 8, 9, 36, 59, 99, 110
Checker 500, 60
Coca-Cola Badger 300, 34
Coors Light 300, 37

D

Davis, Bill, 24-26
Davis, Dan, 102
Daytona, 66, 69, 75, 97, 98
Daytona 500, 7, 18
Delaware 500, 37

Dickies 500, 86
Die Hard 500, 53

E

Earnhardt, Dale, 6, 31, 51, 53, 55, 60, 61, 62, 64, 65, 69
Earnhardt, Dale Jr., 9, 18, 64, 65, 106
Edwards, Carl, 85, 86, 90

F

Fairgrounds Raceway, 30
Ford 200, 69, 98
Ford 400, 86, 107
France, Bill, 60

G

Gant, Harry, 30, 31, 51, 64, 65
Ginn, Bobby, 102
Goody's 500, 54
Gordon, Jeff, 9, 17, 51, 54-55, 61, 62, 106

H

Homestead-Miami Speedway, 7, 86, 90, 107
Hunter, Jim, 60

I

International Race of Champions (IROC), 12, 57, 58, 66-69, 73, 96
Irvan, Ernie, 53
I-70 Speedway, 26

K

Kansas Speedway, 83
Kenseth, Matt, 9, 64, 65, 86, 87,
    90, 100, 106

L

laps, 16, 17, 24, 51, 53, 54, 70,
    106
Lenox Industrial Tools 300, 5
Locust Grove, 14, 20
Lowe's 250, 69, 98

M

Madison International Speedway,
    37
Martin, Arlene, 75, 78
Martin, Jackie Estes, 15
Martin, Julian, 14-17, 18, 20, 24
Martin, Mark
    ASA Rookie of the Year, 23
    begins driving, 13-14
    begins racing in NASCAR,
        29
    car dealership and museum
        in Batesville, 73-75, 81
    first tries Craftsman Truck
        Series, 69
    500th straight Cup start, 6
    graduation, 21
    moves to Busch Series, 39
    moves to Springfield, 22
    named among Busch Series'
        25 Greatest Drivers,
        64, 65
    named among NASCAR's
        Greatest 50 Drivers, 64
    retirement, 8, 80-81, 87,
        93, 107
    600th straight Cup start, 6,
        7-8, 11
    Sportsman Division track
        champion, 20
    wins Arkansas State
        Championship, 14
    wins Missouri Fairgrounds
        Championship, 21
Martin, Matt, 75, 76-78
MB2, 99, 100, 102
Michigan International
    Speedway, 50, 52
midget-car racing, 76, 77
Miller Genuine Draft 400, 53
Milwaukee Mile, 27
Mountain Dew Southern 500,
    52

N

Nashville International Raceway,
    30
New Hampshire International
    Speedway, 6
New Smyrna Beach Raceway,
    22
North Wilkesboro Speedway,
    69, 98

O

Old Dominion 500, 30

P

Peterson, Steve, 33, 35-36
Phoenix International Raceway, 106
pit stop, 5, 43, 67, 70, 74, 84, 87
points standings, 12, 23, 31, 32, 34, 54, 58, 59, 60, 61, 80, 85, 90, 93, 98, 100, 106, 107, 110
pole positions, 11, 26, 30, 35, 36, 62, 70
Pontiac Excitement 400, 60
prize money, 24, 26, 30, 35

Q

Queen City Speedway, 24, 27

R

racing team, 7, 30, 32, 39, 41, 42, 46, 75, 86, 107
Ragan, David, 96
Redbud 300, 24
Riverside International Raceway, 32
Roush, Jack, 7-9, 12, 39-43, 46-48, 58, 60, 80, 90, 93, 99, 102, 103

S

Signore, Jay, 67
Slick 50 300, 6
Slinger Speedway, 34
Smith, Geoff, 99

Smith, Regan, 100, 102
sponsorship, 7, 30, 31, 33, 39, 91
Stewart, Tony, 61, 84, 90

T

Talladega, 53, 83, 98
TranSouth 500, 33
Trickle, Dick, 23, 25
truck racing, 47, 57-58, 69-70, 93, 96-98, 103
Tryson, Pat, 41, 43, 84

U

U.S. Army, 99
Unser, Al Jr., 69

V

Viagra, 73,

W

Wallace, Rusty, 6, 23, 25, 51, 53, 55, 62, 64, 81, 90
Waltrip, Darrell, 30, 31, 51, 62, 64, 65
Watkins Glen, 16, 49, 50, 52
Winchester Speedway, 35
Winston West 500, 32
World Cup 400, 26
Wrangler SanforSet 400, 30